DISCOVERING
BUTTERFLIES

DOUGLAS
FLORIAN

ALADDIN BOOKS

Macmillan Publishing Company   New York
Collier Macmillan Publishers   London

Every butterfly begins its life inside a very small egg. Sometimes this egg is near many other eggs; sometimes it is alone.

The eggs in this picture were planted by a Tortoise Shell butterfly under a willow leaf, protected from the rain and from wasps or birds that might eat them.

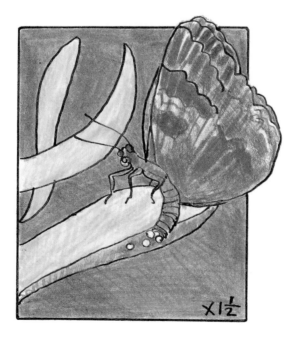

×1

From the egg a tiny caterpillar, or *larva*, hatches by eating through its own eggshell. Then it begins to feed on the plants nearby—but only certain plants. If they are not available, the larva will starve to death before eating other plants.

The Tiger Swallowtail caterpillar shown here is eating the leaf of a cherry tree.

The caterpillar spends almost all of its time eating. When it grows too big for its skin, it splits open its old skin and crawls out wearing a new, larger skin. This process is called *molting*, and it usually happens four or five times before the caterpillar is fully grown.

The caterpillar can bend and turn while eating because its body is divided into thirteen parts or segments.

This Zebra Longwing, shown at one and one-half times its real size, is feeding on the leaf of a passion flower.

x 1½

One day the caterpillar stops growing. It attaches itself to a leaf or stem with a small button of silk it has spun. Now it is a *pupa*. It lets its skin harden into a shell.

This pupa, a brownish color, looks like a dead leaf and so does not attract the attention of birds that might eat it.

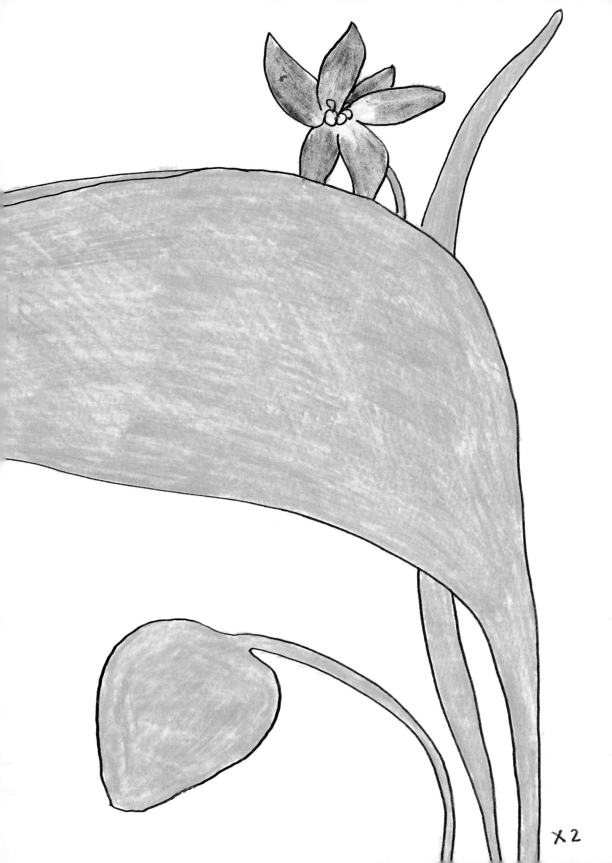

X2

x 8

Inside the shell the caterpillar is growing wings and six long, thin legs. When all the changes are complete, the shell is split open and out comes a butterfly.

This Brimstone butterfly has expanded its wings by pumping blood into them. Now it must let the wings dry and harden before it can fly.

A real Brimstone is only this big.

A butterfly's head has two eyes (A), a pair of antennae (B), which help its balance, touch, and smell, and a long tongue (C) called a *proboscis*. It is coiled up when at rest and uncoiled to drink nectar from flowers.

The middle area of the body is the *thorax* (D). The butterfly's six legs (E), two forewings (F), and two hindwings (G) are attached to the thorax. The delicate wings are covered with rows of brightly colored scales (H) that overlap one another like roof tiles.

In the *abdomen* (I) are the butterfly's breathing holes and organs for digestion and reproduction. (This is a Copper butterfly.)

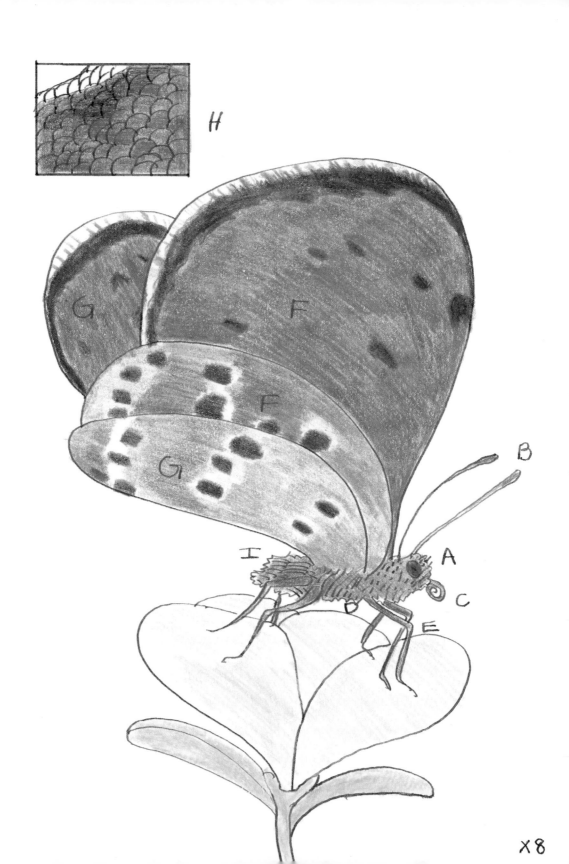

Butterflies have been on earth for about 150 million years. Today there are about 20,000 kinds or *species* of butterflies. New species are discovered every year. They live all over the world, except in Antarctica. The greatest number of species are found in the tropics.

Some butterflies spend most of their time alone. Others are seen in groups. Sulphur butterflies gather around puddles or moist ground.

X1

X I

Some butterflies have colors or features that protect them by blending into places where they live. This African Dry-leaf butterfly looks like a dry, dead leaf.

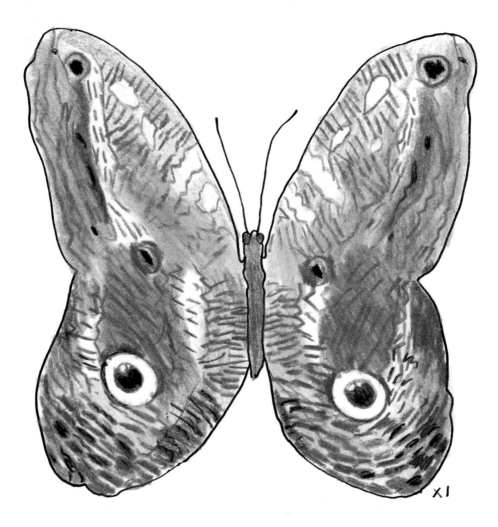

The spots on the wings of this Owl butterfly look like
the eyes of an owl.

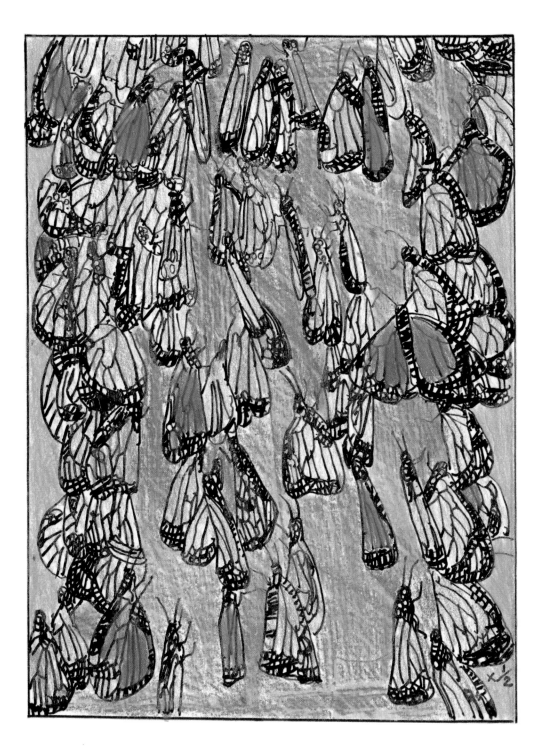

Many butterflies cannot live in cold weather. Some that spend summer in cooler areas move, or *migrate*, to warmer places in the fall.

Monarch butterflies migrate from Canada and northern United States to Florida, California, and Mexico. There they rest from their long journey, sometimes thousands of them on one tree.

Just as there are differences in the way people look, there are variations between butterflies of the same species. These two Tiger Swallowtails have very different colorings and markings.

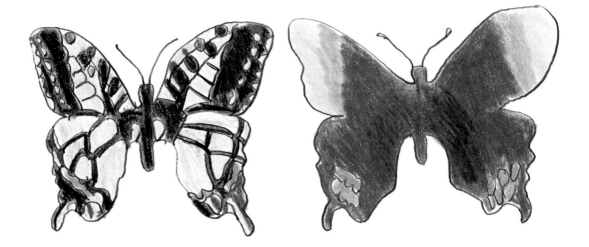

The male Brimstone is a bright yellow while the female is an ivory white.

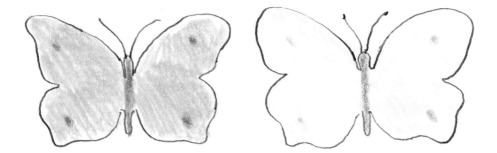

When butterflies of a species live in different places, they often have different markings, like these three kinds of Apollo butterflies.

The color of the Map butterfly depends on when it is born. Those born in the spring are orange-red with black markings. The ones born in the summer are mostly black with light yellow or white spots.

Here are some of the most beautiful butterflies in the world. These three Rajahs live in central Africa.

x 1½

The giant Morpho is a bright metallic blue. This tiny Hairstreak is as small as a penny. They are both found in South America.

The butterflies in the rest of this book are all found in North America. White butterflies are usually white, but they may have marks of black, brown, blue, or yellow. Whites sometimes travel hundreds of miles to find a warmer climate.

Swallowtails are the largest butterflies of North America. The long shapes at the bottom of their wings are called tails. Swallowtails are often found near flowers.

x1

The Painted Lady has many spots and lines of color.

One of the few butterflies that prefers the shade of the woods is the Admiral. Its white stripes look like the stripes on a navy admiral's uniform.

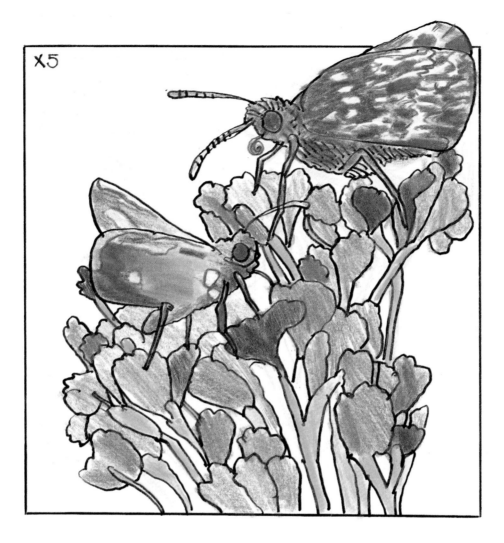

Skippers are brown or orange and brown. They have fatter bodies than most butterflies. They have small wings and can fly very fast. The Skippers in the picture are five times as big as real ones.

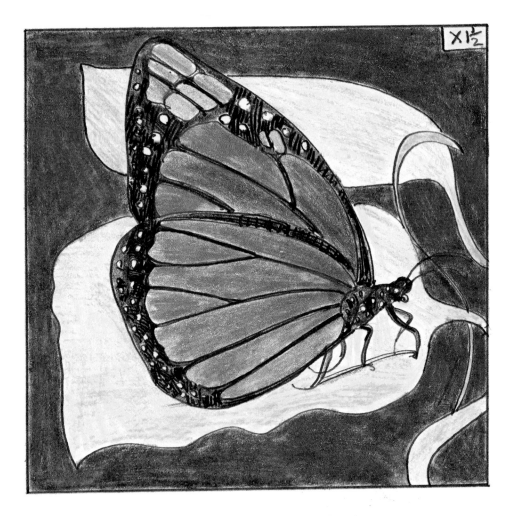

The Monarch is large and brightly colored. Birds don't like to eat Monarchs because they taste bad. Monarchs fly more slowly than most butterflies.

Copper butterflies are usually colored like a copper pot. They are fast fliers and hard to catch. You can find them in meadows and alongside country roads.

The Blue is usually colored blue—but sometimes it is brown or white!

Butterflies are valuable to us. By carrying a flower's pollen from place to place, they help new flowers grow. Because butterflies are very sensitive to their surroundings, scientists study them to see if an environment is becoming unhealthful. With their great variety of colors and shapes, butterflies add beauty to our world.

Each year there are fewer butterflies. They are harmed by pollution and by the destruction of their living places or *habitats*. Let's try to protect them.

FROM TOP: Malachite, Comma, Hairstreak, Orangetip, Leafwing

To Marie

Aladdin Books
Macmillan Publishing Company
866 Third Avenue, New York, NY 10022
Collier Macmillan Canada, Inc.
First Aladdin Books edition 1990
Printed in the United States of America
A hardcover edition of *Discovering Butterflies* is available from Charles Scribner's Sons,
Macmillan Publishing Company.

10 9 8 7 6 5 4 3 2 1

Library of Congress Cataloging-in-Publication Data

Florian, Douglas.
Discovering butterflies/Douglas Florian. — 1st Aladdin Books ed.   p.   cm.
Reprint. Originally published: New York: Scribner, © 1986.
Summary: Describes the structure, life cycle, and behavior of butterflies and depicts different species
found in North America, Africa, and South America.
ISBN 0-689-71376-2
1. Butterflies — Juvenile literature. [1. Butterflies.] I. Title.
[QL544.2.F58 1990]
595.78'9 — dc20   89-37816   CIP   AC